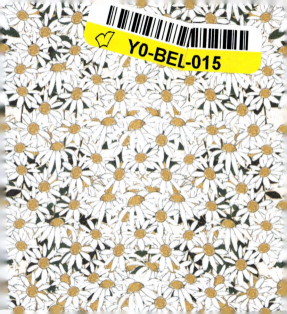

For My Dear Friend,

With Love, From

© 1999 Havoc Publishing
Artwork © 1999 Teresa Kogut

ISBN 0-7416-1116-3

Published by Havoc Publishing
San Diego, California

Made in China

www.havocpub.com

Havoc Publishing
9808 Waples Street
San Diego, California 92121

You are a beary special friend...
May our affection never end.
You do so much for me,
You are a special person, I can see!

A friend who provides

Love and caring, and never hides

What is inside the heart

Is a friend from the start.

Friendship is a gift,
It gives our spirits a lift.
It makes each day brighter,
And makes our spirits lighter.

My friend has touched my soul
Made my life complete and whole.
My friend is certainly a blessing;
For this, my gratitude I'm expressing.

A HUG

is just

an "H" and a "G"

with "U"

in the middle.

In the garden of our dreams,
Friends can fill our nights
with moonbeams,
And make each day brighter
and beautiful,
And our hearts more full.

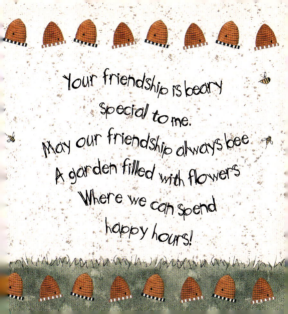

Your friendship is beary
special to me.
May our friendship always bee
A garden filled with flowers
Where we can spend
happy hours!

Shopping is sometimes a chore,
Planning and cooking a bore.
But when these things are done
with a friend,
The time passes quickly and the
happiness doesn't end.

You are so beary special to me,

A friend who takes time to bee,

Someone who shares, cares and gives,

And that's what makes me so appreciative.

Roses are red,

Violets are blue.

Though it's often unsaid,

Our friendship is true.

Friends do so much for us,

A simple call to say, "I care," and, "Hello."

To catch up, chat and discuss

What's in our hearts, they seem to know.

Oh, dear friend of mine,

You'll never know how much you provide.

You make the world a better place,

And you always put a smile on my face.

A best friend brightens your day with the sweet things she says.

The love that my friend
shares with me
Makes all that I dream
possible to be!

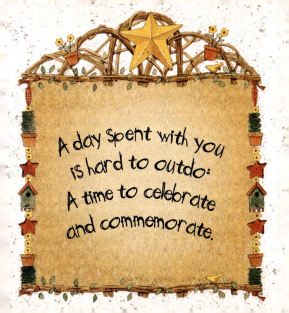

A day spent with you
is hard to outdo:
A time to celebrate
and commemorate.

If we are all musical notes,

With our friends we make up a

beautiful song.

When we decide to devote

Our time to composing,

our friendship can be lifelong.

I used to sit and pretend
That I would someday find a friend
Who would share my joys and tears
And help chase away my fears.
In you, my friend, I have found
Someone whose love knows no bounds
And I thank the stars each day
For all the happiness that's come my way.

In this garden, there's a lily

Offering companionship.

It's a symbol of our friendship,

And how happy we'll always be.

Our friendship
is like a daisy, filled
with yellow sunshine,
which brightens
every day.

In the darkest of days,
You are sunshine and light.
There are so many ways
That you make my
world bright.

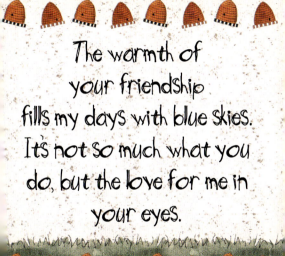

The warmth of
your friendship
fills my days with blue skies.
It's not so much what you
do, but the love for me in
your eyes.

Friends are like pansies
Growing in the garden.
Each guarantees
That it is special to the other,
And as necessary as sunshine
and water.

With the love you bestow,
It seems that with friendship,
you reap what you sow.
The more care you put in,
The greater the respect and
affection you win.

Flowers are like friends,
Full of beauty, end to end.
Each petal a memory
Of their shared history.

Friends fill our days
and hours
With blue skies and flowers.
Each minute filled with fun,
And days filled with sun.

A hug is best when given by a true friend.

As long as I keep
you in my heart,
as friends we will
never be apart.

When I count up
the things that are nice,
I have to count
my friend twice.

A friend loves us for who we are,

Not what we do, or how we appear.

A friend understands

That we are unique,

We are special in our own ways,

Like a precious antique.

Even when we are apart,
I keep my friend in my heart.
When my friend is in my thoughts
we are close,
And that's important because my
friend matters most.

Stars are for wishing. There are millions of stars in the sky, and wishes can go on forever. But a friend like you is my wish fulfilled.

Friends
bring sunshine,
laughter and happy
thoughts to our
lives.

To sit and talk of
unimportant things
Is always comforting
When we can spend
that day in the
company of a friend.

Friendship
BEARS all things.

I Corinthians 13:7

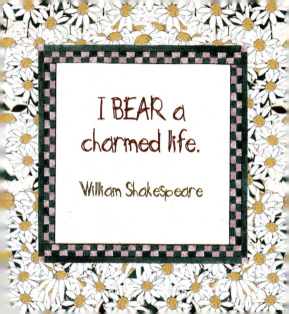

I BEAR a charmed life.

William Shakespeare

Poppies represent sunshine
and happy days with friends.
Friendship with you is divine.
May our friendship never end.

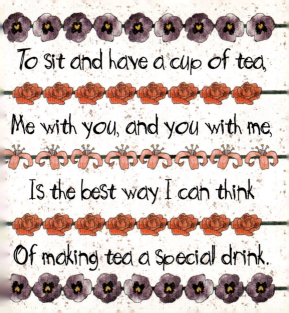

To sit and have a cup of tea,

Me with you, and you with me,

Is the best way I can think

Of making tea a special drink.

Flowers of
true friendship
never fade.

American Proverb

My friend is always there to lend

a helping hand.

I know no matter what, my friend

will understand.

Many secrets my
friend has heard,
And not uttered
a word.

A friend
stands by you
and helps to
guide you.

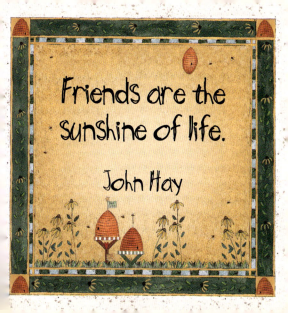

Friends are the
sunshine of life.

John Hay

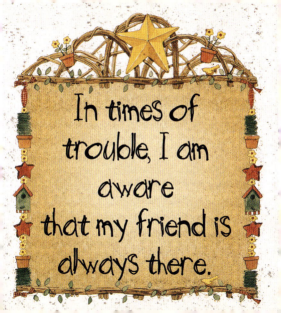

In times of trouble, I am aware that my friend is always there.

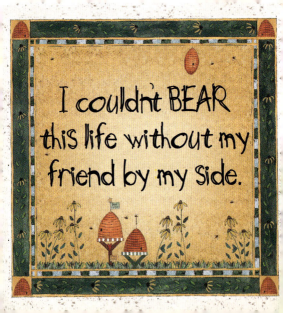

I couldn't BEAR this life without my friend by my side.

Our friendship's
never ending,
My love to you I'm sending.
These wishes come
your way
Because you've been a
special friend each day.

To share our hopes and
dreams
Is often a hard thing to do,
But we know a friend takes
wishes as they seem,
Because a friend helps to
make them come true.

When we are sad and blue,
And we are weighted down
by our troubles,
We know a friend who is true
Will find a way to give
happiness that doubles.

Happiness comes from time spent together. Friendship from the heart. Memories from time together.

For my friend I would go anywhere.
I would travel the world, or the
deepest sea.

My friend is one who is known to
care and my friend gives love and
respect to me.

There is so much that we share:

Love, friendship and care.

The best times are spent with you near.

We're friends for always, that's clear!

My best friend is the one who brings out the best in me.

Henry Ford

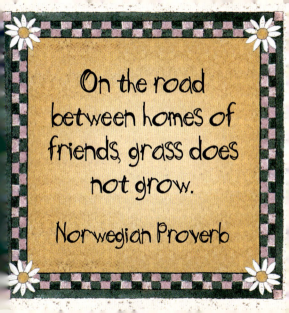

A friend who loves you will BEAR your burdens, and divide them in half by doing so.

My friend is a true friend.
I know this because my friend
brings out the best in me,
and my friend helps me in the
face of adversity.
I know our relationship will
never end!